flight

flight

poems
by

Katharine Coles

Red Hen Press | Pasadena, CA

Book layout by Selena Trager

Library of Congress Cataloging-in-Publication Data

Names: Coles, Katharine.
Title: Flight : poems / by Katharine Coles.
Description: Pasadena, CA : Red Hen Press, [2015]
Identifiers: LCCN 2015038702 | ISBN 9781597099929 (softcover : acid-free paper)
Classification: LCC PS3553.O47455 A6 2015 | DDC 811/.54—dc23
LC record available at http://lccn.loc.gov/2015038702

The Los Angeles County Arts Commission, the National Endowment for the Arts, the
Pasadena Arts & Culture Commission and the City of Pasadena Cultural Affairs Division,
the Los Angeles Department of Cultural Affairs, Dwight Stuart Youth Fund, Sony Pic-
tures Entertainment, and Ahmanson Foundation partially support Red Hen Press.

First Edition
Published by Red Hen Press
www.redhen.org

acknowledgments

The author gratefully acknowledges the following publications, in which some of these poems first appeared: *Able Muse*: "Dog Days," "Found Objects"; *The Antioch Review*: "Eve," "Heat Wave"; *Ascent*: "Faultline," "Happiness"; *Axon*: "At the Museum of Musical Instruments," "Virgil's Tomb"; *DIAGRAM*: "Poems 2.0," "Refraction," "The Thing Is"; *bateau*: "Less to See, More to Fear"; *Gargoyle*: "Pancake Batfish"; *The Gettysburg Review*: "All Souls Night," "All Souls Night for Inanimate Objects," "Winter Solstice"; *Mead*: "Love Note," "Metaphysical"; *Narrative*: "February 14th"; *North Dakota Review*: "The Body Is No Scientist.," "Subtraction"; *PANK*: "Hotel Mercure," *Poet Lore*: "So Far North"; *Poetry Northwest*: "Interiority," "Resolved," "Imaginary Numbers"; *The Southwest Review*: "Glass House"; *Sugarhouse Review*: "Blue," "Camera Obscura," "Sumatran Lilies," "Trail Guide"; *upstreet*: "Thirty Years with These Lions"; *Valparaiso Poetry Review*: "Collector," "Hawks."

"Eve" was reprinted on the Best American Poetry web site, December 12, 2009. "All Souls Night" was reprinted in Best Spiritual Writing, 2012. "Out Like a Lion" was published on line, in video, and in audio as part of the Bite-sized Poem Project. "Imaginary Numbers" owes a particular debt to Barry Mazur's thrilling explanation, in *Imagining Numbers*, of why these strange beasts are not only possible but inevitable. Any lack of clarity in this poem is mine alone and can be remedied by reading his beautiful book. "The Evidence Is Piling Up," "The Body Is No Scientist.," and "Amen" were written in conversation, through poems and other means with Don Share.

Most of the poems in this manuscript arose directly or indirectly from a project, "Natural Curiosities," in my ongoing collaboration with visual artist Maureen O'Hara Ure. I am most grateful to the University of Utah Research Committee and the office of the Vice President for Research, which generously supported this work through a Research and Creative Grant Award.

Last but never least, my heartfelt thanks go out to the many people who have supported me in different ways during the writing of this book, including but not limited to my husband Chris Johnson, Melanie Rae Thon, Charles Hood, the whole Coles family, and finally Kate Gale, Mark Cull, and all the fancy birds in the Red Hen flock.

contents

1 ⁓ glass house

II ~ found objects

1   glass house

Hotel Mercure

I could say you loom
And you would. Could reach
My hand to touch you—

Lucid swimmer, slick
Whipper snapping through
My window's dark. Forgive me:

Could *almost* reach. Moon,
Remember that hotel-
In-the-round, spinning

Us through the Paris night? You
Used it as your mirror, every hall
Curving out of sight, into

Geometry's continuous now. How
Did they slice our room? Pie-
Eyed, I recall

Only the bed, too small
For any one. Cheap wine, loaf, a living
Up to an idea. Surely

We were happy? *In time,*
In time. And you?
You haven't aged a bit.

Refraction

Because time passes more slowly
In water than in air, everything

Floats, muscle,
Memory, and bone all
Anything but light. I take

My time, roundabout
Detour and angle, to get
To the point. Even

Into your arms. Did you know
A single point of light departs a crystal

In so many directions
At once—say tepee, say traffic cone,

Say sorcerer's hat glammed with stars—
Both straight and wayward? Oh,

My searchlight, consider the mathematician
Noodling around like any poet
Daydreaming the improbable, then

All at once stumbling over
Something useful. Not yet—
Centuries from now. Still,

What's a dreamer, only ever
After beauty, to do? Rub her eyes,

Bemused. Shuck her jammies,
Check her watch, go out
For beer. I am on the verge

Every moment of mislaying
Credit card, laptop, wits. Even

You, my *bête blanc*, my obstacle,
My great good dirigible, my distraction: I ask,

How do we live in this world,
Knowing only everything we do?

Swoon

Under the roof a bird sings out the day,
Full-throated among mosaic trees

Her voice could draw to fruit. Heaven glitters,
Inlaid. She's lost her way. Between

Creation and the arch it echoes,
Time won't end
                              nor what we can picture:

A sky assembled, a pelican
Gone to sea, a dog turned demon pitched across
Limits we imagine.
                              Anything

Winged may fly—a lion, the dead.
And then the infant, bird in hand at last,
Child fingers holding so hard

We want to peel them back.
                                        The child is paint
On plaster. The trapped bird calls
Again, again. A human lifetime later

Two dogs under the table worry
Their conventional bone. Silver changes hands

And twelve men raise their cups.

                              We paint the animals
Kinder than we are. We paint each other

So: patient, able
To sleep in any nook, to hold a bird

Or suckle from a wolf, speaking
Our own language. The charcoal stick.
The wash of paint on plaster. This world

Won't give up arching to catch the light,
And the bird flutters in its panic,
Its body, like ours, beating against the walls.

San Marco's Floors

Only years later

Will I remember to look down. Eyes not
Undazzled yet by golden ceilings
But half-accustomed, ready

To stray. And so, crossed
By centuries of boots, peacocks draggle tails
And blackbirds poise in windless branches
Imagined a sea away, re-imagined here

And here. Every little bird means something
If only to itself. How like me to forget
What holds me, to believe everything uplifting
Lives in the rafters. See here

A pair of crimson lions laid in stone, gazing upward,
Hopeful as my old dogs, to meet my eyes.

Thirty Years with These Lions

I have seen them in Taipei guarding
Museum steps, in Kamakura temples

Guarding their own myth, winged and guarding
Time's passage at San Marco. Excavated,

In Istanbul's galleries they become
Inscrutable the further they erode. Once,

We took our lions literally. They stalked
Our caves and dogged our steps before

We posed them. We knew, if we lay down, just
What we were doing, what it meant

To invite them in. I don't know why
We set them in stone. Take my neighbor,

Her tiny bungalow. Her husband dead,
She placed these lions to flank her

Abbreviated walkway, a gate between them
Though she has no fence. Their heads, curled

Locks flowing European-style, almost reach
Her eaves. As if they might protect her

Just by looming. In their calm, they keep

Confusion at bay, the local toughs, his ghost. Look

At that paw, its delicate lift, claws
Retracted for the long moment. Ninety

Last summer. Sharp, still ready, she moves
Off her porch to draw me through the gate.

At Pompeii

Thunder gathers. Off-season, the place almost empty, but for the guide who knows too much for his little clutch of tourists and me.

As usual, I don't want to listen, except when that bird sings.

And that one.

I go in every little room, until I'm left behind.

What have I heard about wind's fickleness? This wind could be blowing from the farthest reaches of sky, it is so persistent.

A pair of lizards flickers by, brilliant green, one chasing, then the other. From everywhere, I see the mountain in its shift of clouds.

Roads intact. Another room. Someone knows every rock, when they all come down. Where they fall

They look like any graveyard, so I don't know the graveyard when I see it, also ruined.

Those lizards—was it love or play?

In this dark corner a painted bird glows and glows. Crimson stroke, blue feather, tail spirited open. That singing.

All day I am living on the skins of my eyes.

Inside my head, a voice takes hold.

Metaphysical

—Herculaneum

1. New walls. Old walls. Suspended
Between them: me

On a bridge, thinking of home. So words
Fly across the ocean—old friends—

And land on my tiny screen:
An invitation. From the marsh below

Frogs call too, voluptuous.
Not to me. If they dig,

They don't seek the past. Yesterday,
In the museum, I saw frogs

Carved of stone, football-sized, mouths
Wide open. As if someone, hearing

These, wanted to let something out,
Something in. Heartbreak. A fly. How

Could I divine what some sculptor meant
So long ago? Much less these frogs.

2. And how could I have thought anybody
Could read anyone else? *No less*

Than three, I overhear. *That was*
The number of the Graces. And

No more than nine. Muses? Magic
Equation I will never know. Lovers,

Glasses of wine. Here is
What they made, painstaking

In tiny tiles and brushstrokes. Which nature—
Old drama queen—covered over

And men dug out again to look at
Millennia later, still

Fresh. Dogs like my dog
Scratching, chasing. A snake

Corkscrewing—wine again, on
The brain—and a sky-blue lintel. What

They found beautiful, I find beautiful.
A wet nose. A singing frog. A glass

Round enough to let the grape breathe.
Nobody ever meant these flowers,

Little yellow stars, to burst from walls
And stairwells. But they do.

Less to See, More to Fear

Bat Cave Temple, Bali; Sydney Botanical Gardens

1.   Through gates and pavilions, under
The elaborate architecture of human attention
Carved with bats and snake gods' open maws,

The actual bats, millions, tuck themselves in
To sleep this too-bright afternoon away, until

Luminous dark opens to their humming.
The cave opens the sacred mountain,

Miles into its heart, a ravenous dream
                                    you could enter, slipping
Under drowsing shadows, through guano stink,

Past the real python, huge, unlidding
Chilly eyes to yawn, jaw unhinged,
Tongue tasting you, that hiss of pleasure,
                                    and feel

The mountain's whole weight—

(2. Here, the stench recalls them—flying foxes
Hung high in open treetops. Fox-sized
Bodies rolled into wings so orange I mistook them

For huge, stinking fruit, until one peeled
Himself open—)

Pancake Batfish

Could be a character in a nonsense poem
Or one of those arbitrary word pairs the *Times*

Makes you type in when you email an article—*dragoons*
Reluctantly, 18-room verandah, Hindu

Transportation. Something about
Security, what a human can do and a machine

Can't.
      Automata be.
          Pancake batfish could be
A title my husband the whimsical scientist

Assigns me.
      It is, in fact, this bottom-
Dwelling creature, for the first time named

On the front page, its newly Googleable image
Pushing up batty on little legs, a missing link goggling

Indignant eyes at our invading camera
Run by remote control from another world,

We are in so deep. Its mouth, red as Marilyn's,
Opens a cartoon grimace.
      Click here: not annoyed, it pancakes

Itself flat against the sandy bottom. *Here*: its eyes
Are bluer than my own, more beautiful, blind and farther

Seeing. Its whole body, this specimen held between
Anonymous thumb and forefinger, is smaller

Than my ear's inside curve. Its colors didn't survive
Its journey to our surface, organs

Blown when the pressure drops
Too far. What wonders are we missing? All taken

Before, of course, in waters murked
Only by their depths—so deep and dark we send

Adventurers, send machines that fix
Nothing we can ruin, extend our coldest eye

And numbest hand—our emissaries look and probe,
Collect and transmit back. The creature

Has been there for millennia. We see it
This first time from a distance, and in passing.

—Gulf of Mexico, May 2010

So Far North

The birds do not sing
Even during the day

Don't announce their doings
In their private dark

A black-backed woodpecker
Or the meticulous wind

Hungry from the north
Probes at the trees

And all around this
Perpetual sunrise, one

Rose-lit hour, then blue
Scattered, sourceless, cold

Love Note

Helsinki, December

So far north, noon slips its light
Angling under the clouds, a sleight

To draw city and harbor out of themselves
Into a fragile wash of grey and mauve
Ten wings beat at, rasping the air.
So five swans ruffle the water:

Young near grown, still mottled;
The pair, stark, too bright to look at.
December. The sun, hardly risen, falls.
My hand lies with his in his dark pocket

Where I will slip this note for him to find.
You, it says. *You*. I find in him
The world I ride, poised, so gently turning
I can't feel it shift around its fulcrum

(Any more than I feel my mind move me)

Toward the light I'm given. Today's glance,
Muted, here unbearably brief, scorches
The southern hemisphere, burns itself out
In the profligate orchid's ruffed throat;

On the nectar bat's four-inch, tongue, furred,
Its anchor buried so deep in its sternum

It eats its heart out among the flowers;
Or—what on earth?—in Madagascar's

Moth, iridescent, light-footing a feathered wing,
Rolling out its harpoon proboscis, barbing
The eyelid gently, not to wake the robin—
So I'm fallen, hooked, into such passion,

Sipping and sipping a mineral dream of tears
That, in slaking, just reignites my thirst.

Blue

Figure 1: Increasing detail of a Morpho butterfly wing tells a
more interesting and informative story than just one image.
—Photographer Felice Frankel, *Nature*

No dyes but only surface could create
That shimmering texture, taffeta

Or opal—stone's cool burn
Repeated in material so fragile

It crumbles at a touch. The opal's
Fragile too, for rock. Zooming in,

Felice's camera sees *the wings*
Are mirrors. Magnified

Step by step to visibility
Even my poor eye can see, they lose

Gorgeous iridescence, and become
Structures for reflection. Also

Gorgeous, though Felice
Talks about what they tell us,

Not their beauty. I heard about
A butterfly in New England

That feasts all spring on violets. Perhaps
A myth. But the Karner Blue

Eats its fill of lupine, and digests,
Then opens wings to let

The flower fly. Who says
There is no magic

In the world?—the sky
Unfolds upon the day; the lake,

Becalmed on quiet afternoons,
Makes the sky its own

And gives it back. And if love lights
My evenings into deeper nights,

My eye, no matter my
Reflections, what I devour,

Returns to him: refracting,
Scattered, only partly true.

Song at the Museum of
Musical Instruments

My love gave me a golden harp, he did,
Bowed like a boat to fly me under sail,
A horn shaped like a cunning chickadee,
A drum hollowed out of a human head.

Bowed like a harp, I flew under his sail,
Fretted like a fiddle inlaid with pearl.
Some things never drummed into my head
Until now. My love and I grow older.

He frets. He fiddles. I lie. I knit and pearl.
We're picking up and heading for the boneyard.
Oh, now my love and I are growing older
He carves me a trumpet from a femur

He's picked up, heading from the boneyard.
A robin's skull will whistle any tune,
And he can carve a trumpet from a femur.
I have barely wet my lips and blown

But my skull will carry any tune.
I toot my own horn. Cunning chickadee,
I've barely wet my lips and I am blown.
My love gave me a golden harp. Didn't he?

Collector

One thing beside another with no reason
Beyond some taxonomic hallucination—
Ceylon broach, South African soapstone pipe bowl,

Azurite fetish, scrimshaw hairpin, then
At last a notional order: entire cases of heads,
human here, and shrunken; there

Avian: ear and ruff,
Corythaix persa's crest, showy green
Edged white, or, beyond ornament, beaks

Lamellated, conical, fissirostral, each evolved
Precisely for its function, which
The gloss declines to tell us. In this case

Feet, disarticulated to fix attention
Before we're free to see the birds entire
And frankly disappointing, dusty, posed, not up

To their fantastic names (Ascar fairy bluebird,
Crimson sunbird, ivory-breasted pitta), though to see
Any such creature in full motion, flustering

Deepest canopy, silencing the jungle,
Would be something else again,
It would.

What They Took with Them

Death.

Let me be more specific: strong
Arms. Swords. Horses. Bows and arrows,

Their bloodthirst. Over there, they traded
Souls for souvenirs. A jewel or trinket, an image

Cast and recalled—fire-breathing lions
Woven into tapestries, painted on ceilings, entering

New imagination. Like this cathedral, its shape
Learned by unreliable heart, then

Quarried from the limestone hill, interior hollowed
Out stone by stone, so all the light to lead us

Falls from heaven into earth, flinging our long
Shadows to the floors. Years spent

Estranged, they dreamed of home, memory
Reshaping steep little streets, time wearing

All the old faces, until they returned
Unknown. They carried back with them

An idea, an emptiness. And changed everything.

St. Emilion/The Crusades

Hunt

Mosaic Museum, Constantine's Palace, Istanbul

1. Lion beating expectations
In a doe's jugular.

2. Marten with sparrow
Tucked into its mouth.

3. *What is dismembered by art?*
What by time?—Good shepherd lugging

4. His sheep, the only animal pictured
Always prey, away

5. From what's *Out there*. I stalk
Barbs and thickets, all

6. In two dimensions. No
Digging down, no flight. Surface

Chipping away.
     7. At my hotel
All night I hear chortling

Through walls, from the fire escape,
Throaty pleasure. *Did you know*

8. *The stag will eat the snake*
Twining his neck and body? Stag

Immune to venom. The artist,
Lost to all but this, shows us,

9. Meticulous, so many lost, even man
Torn by bears. 10. Big cat. 11. None remains

12. Intact. *Would you rather*
Not know? Scuff slippers

13. Over winged hybrid, floored,
Lopsided, goat-horned. Gnaw

Your own haunches bloody.
Look: you at last

14. Sated, face full of holes,
Pulse ticking

15. Tile by jeweled tile, body half
Eaten alive this time.

The Evidence Is Piling Up

A wallet on the seat. A jet trailing
Its excesses behind it

Like some raggedy kite.
But where's the history detective?

Where is the forensic scientist
With her dandy tube of lipstick?

Where, in all of this,
Is the body? Once,

It threw itself between you
And any old hole in the ground.

The thing we can't name
We can't see, whatever

The writing on the walls,
Whatever goddamn stink it makes.

The Pocket Inside

First it was simple. A pocket inside a pocket
For a key, a coin to feed the meter, something

You could get at easily with two fingers
Without plunging your whole hand in. Anyone

Could see it. Everyone knew what
You kept there. Then it became a secret

Safe for the journey, zipped and Velcroed,
Tucked in a seam or a waistband or up

A poet's exiled cuff, though it hides
No poems. You may find a credit card in it,

A coded message, a document forged to get you
Out of a country or in, but nothing to say

I am here, I love you. Nothing you can blow
Your nose on or wave or wear on your sleeve,

Like that language from a small country
For so long hidden under the tongue of history

It holds a thousand words
For memory, none for imagination.

Glass House

Outside, rhododendrons keep their season,
Tumbling into fullest flower, blown
Purple, yellow, white with throats blazed scarlet,

While inside we stalk the reclusive orchid
Collected a world away, clinging here
To the tree grown for it; costus dubius;

Peer at the psychotria bacteriophilia,
Berries popping crimson in the shadows

Little tricks of the eye.

I don't even know what I am seeing.
Around every corner I catch my reflection;

Under leaf and vine again I glimpse you
Slipping between the branches, searching
This museum of the impossible

For the flower shaped like a pitcher, an ear
Cupped only for your voice. Breath weights the air.
Should I turn around? Should I follow?

Camera Obscura

Invention fills the gap.
The blacked-out room—Dear Heart—
Recasts a radiant street,
Buses flashing past.

My heart's a room darkened
Beyond memory,
Your kisses flashing past,
Discrete packets of light.

Beyond memory,
Even my words to you,
Discreet, pack up light
To build a world from need—

My words to you can even
Break the poem's heart.
To build a world, you need
To draw the curtains. The poem's

Dark heart breaks
Under light's prick.
Draw the curtains. The dark's
A mirror, amnesiac.

Through a pinprick, light
Casts the world, radiant.
When the mirror forgets,
Invention fills the gap.

Hagia Sophia

If my eye climbs
Red ladders to the sky—scaffolding

Has closed the balconies,
So the stairs—those angels flew

Themselves up there. My camera sees
Light arrowing discrete

Beams from narrow windows,
Diffusing again when I look

Naked-eyed. So,
Seraphim. No body, face

Rubbed out by an idea, all wing
Fluttering cold fury that cannot

Tell you it's alive
In any sense. Or that any god

Can live here, given
Invocation, addition, sub-

Traction of body, sign—mihrab
And altar both pointing

Toward holy cities rising, human
Mind shrinking everything

To its size. Gabriel's
Body glitters, what's left of it,

And Christ's, and the emperor's
Kneeling. Outside, over the doors,

You can still catch the virgin
Face intact, first glimpsed

In the mirror placed to make you think
She's right before you, then

Reminding you to see
You have to turn around.

Virgil's Tomb

Naples

Pay them no mind, just look and pass on.

It's not, of course, his. This monument. Though

It's not necessarily empty either. If there are bones

Nobody knows whose. If there were ever bones

They are dust. Something

Always stands for something else, this time

Anonymous. Which doesn't mean he isn't here,

Overlooking the bay with me, from under some

Nearby piece of dirt. Unmarked. We are both

Breathless then. I climb to feel my own

Heartbeat. *Enjoy the view.* So quiet

I hear gulls, can almost hear waves

Shifting below. *Just the Sunday traffic.* Find

A little company. *Ave*, whoever you are.

The sea always changing, the same as ever.

Between the Lines

Darwin wrote that our imperfect fossil record is like a book preserving just a few pages. . . . What hope can then be offered to the flesh and blood amidst the slings and arrows of such outrageous fortune?
—Stephen Jay Gould

What is this urge to keep a secret
Life folded so long between the sheets

Then tell it? Lines
We can barely read, a few words, letters sent

To this haphazard future. The airplane I ride
Drags its shadow behind, a give-away

Though field and stone erode
The plane's image and reshape it

Like any mirror of water or air. My face
Is no less mine than ever, but I forget

To see it in the glass. Brushing my teeth,
I'm too busy looking for something

I don't already know. If
Over the years there came a moment

Somebody glanced and thought it perfect
As it was, that moment passed me by.

II 🪶 found objects

Lost In Thought

In the air before her
As if her eyes could reach through

And recover something
Just out of earshot, on the tip of—

Blown galaxy, deep grove—
She's only moving

Farther, the way
One thing keeps on

Leading to another, making
Past and present equal,

Each square marked off
In time. Would she like to escape

This thought? Already wandering
Dark woods, no search party

Coming to find her, no trail
Blazing to show the way.

Found Objects

In the mood of Atget

A skeleton, modeled
Half life size. A bust.
A mounted beetle.
Cultivated dust.

This bat wing, severed
From a life now flown;
Hinge and lever,
Articulated bone—

No: umbrella.
Mooding trumps my eye,
Invents details
To match memory—

A corset, empty
Of the shape it gave,
A passing city,
A fallen nest, a grave.

Say: how do
Your eyes still pin me flat,
When it's you
Laid down in black and white?

Subtraction

The black art of "borrowing" . . . is only a little
more baroque than that of "carrying."
—Steven Stogatz, *The New York Times*

Hard to keep track. Easy to get in trouble. Take
One hand and give to the other, knuckling out
A pocket, snugging a rabbit
Or bauble back into a purse frogged
And glitzed with plastic sequins. One way

You get from whole to half, from promise
To solution, by theft or loss. Drop nothing. Don't
You miss me? Your burden bows your back
Then suddenly lifts. Honest, you only borrow

To stay positive, to keep yourself above
That horizon below which you mustn't
Sink, though at some point you will

Lower yourself. Open your fingers
And give them a flutter, clever filchers, flighty

Little birds you can make light of.

20 Questions

Is it alive?

Does it walk upright?

Does it scavenge?

Can it fly?

Was it recently dug out of the snow?

Buried in debt?

Spotted stitching an organ to its sleeve?

Does it have a favorite jukebox song?

An opposite?

Should we turn and slowly walk away?

If it were a secret, could you keep it?

Aren't you afraid you might forget?

If I showed it to you, would you then?

Shouldn't we turn around?

Is it too late?

Is it bleeding?

Could it be enough?

Have you made excuses?

Can I carry that for you?

Are you sure it's not too late?

Resolved

January 1, 2010

This morning, in dark rooms, people pray
God will reveal himself. And

He does. To those who wish the hardest,
Each his own image: a face

Spotted in a cornflake, an inkblot,
A string of numbers. Through a telescope

Time arrives on the scene; in a dog's entrails,
It peters out. I tell you, this time

If the world wants to leave the decade
Behind a year early, drawn out

By a naught's hopeful emptiness, I say
Good riddance. Even knowing

What happens next, we can't help carving
The lion flopped down with the lamb.

If I showed you a canvas washed
Only in shades of blue, what

Couldn't you see? Though we are
Poor memory's creatures, we have

So many wishes we carve them,
Write them against the sky,

Whisper them, fold them into boats
We launch, lit by small candles,

Onto the river. Sometimes they founder
And sputter close to shore. More often

They drift all the way to the bend
And out of sight, still burning. Can you say

From here which is yours? Make up
Any future you please.

A Dog In Time

Saves nothing. Dips and dodges. Stays
Out all night. Walks akimbo. Snores
Through dog days on her porch. Digs her way
To heaven. Peters out again. Barks

Just so I can hear her, feels delight
Build itself to bursting in her chest.
Has a nose for nuance. Follows news
In passing's present tense with interest,

Tracking sources to their bitter ends.
May or may not follow me. Depends
On where I go. In her own good time
Arrives, waving plumage high. Smiles

To have found me where she is. *Well met*,
Her gallant heart. Shoots. Flies straight. Can't wait.

The Geometry of Dogs

1. My husband, the scientist, insists on
This disclaimer: While the specific theory

Described below may be extensible
To three dogs, four, even fifty-

One dogs (though if you have
Fifty-one dogs on your hands, all

Wagging, rummaging, swishing
Their heads in the trash, higher

Forms of mathematics
Keep you busy) *our* observations

Are limited to *these two* dogs only,
Both large and old now, both still

2. Given to glance sidelong, to mouth
A squeaky toy, or even, on promenade,

To strain a leash and prance, but even more,
Let's face it, inclined to sleep. They do so

Never touching but near enough
To feel each other's breath, sense

A heartbeat, bodies always aligned

3. Exactly parallel

Or perpendicular. Butt-
To-butt, head-to-head, they swivel

Around some mutual axis, one rising
To dig at her bed, then flopping down

Again into that subtle squaring.
4. Dog one, dog two. Tired. True.

The Body Is No Scientist.

1. It wants to live or die without regard to medical evidence.

2. It takes its elixir or spits it out, craves touch and shies away.

3. It won't examine reasons.

4. It loves the slick of butter on its tongue, will suck the marrow in until it pukes, stretches its skin out at noon, and stares at the sun until its sight blazes into dark.

5. Didn't it fall in love with the boy packing his fingers around in a fist?

6. Didn't it lick its wounds into raw meat, then forget?

7. My body runs itself to euphoria and beyond, will run until its knees fray and buckle and its muscles feed on themselves.

8. The clock ticks as if the body attended.

9. Oh, it's petulant, and spoiled, and full of joy, a dumb, petted animal going grey.

10. Even drifting away from itself, lovely, it's no philosopher.

11. It never could count.

Good Heart

Itches, loose patches, spots. Wrist and hip gone
Bony, showing off sprung springs.

My good friend thinks we shouldn't dwell in loss
Of face, little reflected obsessions,

Doesn't want to hear regret from spoiled
Women who never earned a thing like he did.

So he told me, years ago. If he
Meant me, neither of us knew it yet.

Meanwhile, I don't mind my body
Loses luster: hair, breast fallen off from nothing

To write home about. Too late I learned
Nature's axiom, *Youth*

Is beauty, so regret
Ignorance, maybe also biological,

The chance to have enjoyed simply what may
Have been. Will I look back

In twenty years? Lucky then to be
Still here. And here. And here.

February 14

This morning, a house finch sings and bounces
Its bare branch outside our window

Though the sky falls, though snow
Covers the ground. Under the snow

Crocuses swell and the Lenten rose
Already waxes. Our penance

Has yet to begin, our last pulling
Back to eke out meager stores

While we tick off our wrongs. Today,
An old saint signs himself

Yours before losing his head.
And so. Do we

Need an excuse? Our patience
Already ended. Outside,

My husband shovels snow from flower beds
Back onto the drive. Today the birds

Begin mating, I once was told,
Their clear sense of things

Tocking them. This
Little finch, not yet come

Into his plumage, sings
Everything could happen. Wily, every poem

Hatches its little lie. Time changes. Just
Between us, how I like it.

Out Like a Lion

A flock of tiny birds gusts
       Wild—the wind made flesh,
              Feather and hard-flung heart—

And on every pavement beneath
       Vivid glass facades, a body
              A quarter my fist's size

Twists its head
Too far, as if in wonder (the rush:

People step around
       Small death, faces
              Lowered into the gale)—still

Eyes gazing at blue sky
       Reflected so purely she gave
              Over to what moved her,

Believing in her last fling
She could blow right through.

The Tiger Swims

                              because
She wants to. No escape. Eyes wide
Open underwater, paws splayed, swiping—

Who knew they were webbed?—
                              to catch
And hold the lake's power, grin drawn

Wide as any moon with teeth
Bared, a moon any night
Stalking small pulses

Trembling the grass. Equation: one hides,
One seeks. Why

Imagine anything but
Long muscle flowing
Relieved and weightless into the cold?

Cutting My Hair

The head takes its own shape.
Abuzz, clippers shadow
Scalp, curves, nape's
Secretive, tender hollow

Where neck given to skull
Tapers, velvet, down.
Under the stroke, hair falls
Like grass newly mown;

Grazes shoulder and waist,
Strays the curving thighs,
Drifts to rest at last,
Bronze shavings on the tiles—

But no. It's bestial,
Worn naturally as guilt.
Itching, the sheer animal
Undoes her winter pelt.

Orchid House

I would call this one
Lascivious mouth, wide-

Open throat gorging
On itself. This other wears

Petals as a veil, keeps its hunger
Almost secret, though

Inside it's ravenous,
Its perfume holding out

The lure, swoony and dark.
And somewhere hidden

Behind the leaves and blooms
That voice persists—bird,

Exotic cricket, frog singing
Its heart out. As if I spoke

Its extravagant tongue,
An answer to its longing.

Hawk

To be a creature whose one will is life.
Grosbeaks and buntings fuss around the feeder

Of one mind: to eat together and drop
Back into the trees. To be a leaf

Turning under wind, willing
To be shuffled and nosed by bees. Free

Of melodrama. To have no reason
Not to be known. To forget the self.

To give over as moose does to largeness and smell.
To give yourself, like the dogs, to voice

Or the continuous, nuanced alphabet
The weasel's long tail draws across the grass;

Or to be lifted on evening's updraft,
One eye on the ground, heart

Rising with the body, in it, carried—
Nothing to do but hold the body hard;

Nowhere to go but into impossible blue.

Trail Guide

First, follow the Ls—
Lupine to purple larkspur,

Yellow arrow-leaf into
Trilling columbine, warbler

Giving over to
Blur of wings and calliope

Hummingbird coming
To rest tiptoe

Atop a burned-out spruce—
Black and white pelicans

Afloat on the blue air.
Here we are again where

The river won't stop
Throwing itself at the lake.

Look at the man standing
With his rod and creel,

His many-pocketed vest
Festooned with clever lures.

I swear to you, I am
That constant. Anyway,

This is a fool's errand,
Isn't it?—how

One thing gives to another
In its errancy.

Dog Days

Then there are the questions of the body.
What holds it together? What falls
Apart? All of us are faltering, all
In our own ways going rough and shoddy:

My love's arthritic foot and knee; my back
Doubly ruptured, and I was only sitting down.
But these two—they don't think to complain.
They just keep their noses to the track,

Tracking delights of passage, every smell
Of every passerby bearing the *now*
Along in its delicious ripeness, enough.
Could it be enough for us? Leave well

Enough alone, I always say. He says
Every dog has her day every day.

Heat Wave

1. Octet

Brute sun, merciless,
Strafes our lettuces. Gone.

Tender moths strip
Threads asunder, while

Bolt screws tight
Its nut.
        Winged.
                Strong armed.

Ouch, he says.
Come.

2. Envoi

Mercy	Bruit	Mere
Tender	Let	Thread
Mouth	Wing	Armed
Sunder	Strong	Gone

Fault Line

Our mountains ride July, white sails catching,
Troubling the earth. Summer burns the valley,
Drawing green from the spring grasses. Inhale:
Such air could draft flame from an unstruck match.

Over dinner, he spoke what was in my head.
I felt his hand a moment before he touched me.
This morning from my dream the phone pulled me
Calling through my sleep before it sounded—

A long dream, it seemed, whose plot led
Unerring to the ring. So quickly does
The mind construct the ground for its stories.
Take the diamond I wear. His grandmother's, flawed,

It burns around the occlusion at its heart,
And burning becomes the tale it tells, its art.

The Thing Is

                                        you never could leave
Well enough alone. You will never have it made.

Myth operates. Content comes. Design calls and
Who cares? Craft answers to will

Or will to craft. Answer: Who cares?
Operate myth. Come to content. Call design and

Have it made well. Enough. You alone
Could leave. The thing never is.

(beginning with an erasure of a quote by Robert Duncan)

Interiority

The void is not emptiness.

—Deepak Chopra

Not only, *Do I have an inner life,*
Though that too is open

To question, but *Does the universe*
Have one. Call it beauty. Call it

Flick or spin, motion so charming
Someone has to invent it. The nun

Uses words for transportation;
The Buddhist an image he can follow inward,

Riding a syllable's tail. Another
The lash and chain. A comet

Throws itself away on time, and some
Physicist figures where

It goes too deep to see. So brain
Makes peace with mind. *I am,*

They both insist. Until they stop.

Cleo at Fourteen

This morning, my old Aussie's full of joy
And her own compact presence. Spry at heart,
She leads me out, her arthritic canter
Sailing her up the usual path, aslant.

I am full of the past, memory
When she could outrun me every time.
She gambols when a van of dogs drives by
And breaks out, just for her, cacophony.

Against the long grasses she sweeps her sides
And plunges headlong down the shrubbery walk,
A tunnel smelling of deep green and magic.
Later, while I drink my second coffee

She lies on her air conditioning vent. *Oh, dog.*
In her sleep, she wags and wags and wags.

Passage

Afternoon, fall, so late my shadow crosses
Frost-ruined beds, scales the fence, jackknifes over

Into the neighbor's yard—going on
As far as I can see forever. I recall

This day began in sunlight,
Coffee brewing, promise of warmth. I passed

Under my own bare trees to get the news.
Overhead, birds, holding long flight off

As late as they might, opened their bodies
One more time to let the song pass through.

All Souls' Night

Why not shatter a night with snow?—so early—
Or watch a half-moon laze
Back on her bed of clouds, the glitter

Of stars half-crazed by time? Even those
Clouds shred by so fast the moon is left

Hanging onto the night. Planted
On our own ground, we have
The barest sense of each other's bodies

Slipping away. No wonder
We can hardly bear our bliss, pouring

Onto us without a moment's notice—
A tap on the shoulder, a touch, a kiss—
So it fills us up. And it will pass.

All Souls' Night for Inanimate Objects

After Dennis Silk

Anything can be moved. A glass of water
Trembles at my touch. And wind wears
Out that sandstone pillar, grain by grain,

Until it takes a shape that looks, to our eyes,
Like something that might live—a bear, a woman,
A once-bright angel fallen into time.

All it takes. Luck turns on a dime.

Sumatran Lilies

As if flesh were made for thrift instead of spending,
The florist tells me, *When they bloom pinch off*

The stamens, so they don't make a mess of pollen, so
The blossoms, the point of flowering lost, will last.

On my counter, they open, scarlet giving
Over to purple so deep their throats look black,

And breathe out sharp and sweet, filling the room
Until, out of my head, I lose

Heart for amputation. Still, perfume languishes
Down every hall, when we open the front door

Taking us in. Spellbound, we drift through it—the whole
House heavy—and everywhere, cast over carpet

And white linen, brushed onto careless skirt and fingers, find
The brilliant, profligate stain.

Eve

Don't consult the cost.
Rather, mind the body.
Course, occluded, lost

In its heedlessness
It finds itself: too heady
To consult the cost.

Balance grace and dross;
Weigh desire and duty.
Cursed, occult, lost

In this nakedness—
Mea culpa. Steady.
I can't account the cost

Of what I've won. At least
I kept my word. I'd stay
Any course to lose

Everything like this,
To be every body's
Curse. Cut my losses.
I do not mind the cost.

Winter Solstice

Such a long season of grief.
First the fires, then an autumn

Through which light seared every leaf
And dislodged the windows from reflection.

Year by year, everything stays the same.
Moment by moment, everything is changed.

A light flares, goes out, then, somewhere
Almost beyond us, it flares again.

Imaginary Numbers

For Fred Adler

[I]t follows that the Equation has one true Affirmative
Root, two negative ones, and two impossible ones.
—Newton

Whoever applies himself to [mathematics] will believe
there is nothing he cannot understand.
—Cardano, The Great Art

Where *I* becomes
*i*mpossible, the problem

Is no longer the square root,
Or even the negative (through

Brute imagination made
Possible), but both together. Can't imagine?—

Graph. The horizontal line,
Conveys its goods, plus

And minus, into infinity. Simple
Metaphor, leaving time to wonder,

Is infinity's opposite zero? A poet's
Error. Draw

The vertical line. A sort of mirror,
Idlest speculation, trick cabinet

Falsely backed. My friend says
Don't trouble yourself with reality:

Everything exists
Within these walls. Jokester

Mathematician, full
Of irony. And its opposite. A kind

Of magic? Rotate. Again— you've flipped—
And there is *i*, strict, spinning

Simple lines. Without question
A dizzy discipline: a number

Turning into—
Close your eyes. *It's gone.*

Poems 2.0

1. They were in error, of course,
About most things. The clouds

Never were soft. Inside, rambunctious
Then as now, they struck
And swizzled, composing

Pockets of violence,
Electrified. They had
No time to think of being lonely.

2. And the poetry of the earth:
It could cease. We know that now.

3. Flowers, for example, will take
And take, will lash and toothe the air, will

Scatter, and dig in, and rise
Above themselves, and flourish.

4. Do not mistake me. This is
No correction. Don't ask me

5. To count the ways
I have been wrong about love's
Same old la-de-da,

Or how I knew, all along,
I could only betray the flesh

That dazzled me into song.
My own, or his. A poem

6. Might have told us in
So many words. And others.

7. And been wrong.

Amen

She might be singing
And she might be crying. Then again

She might be poring over

Her cookbook or watching the sky
For omens, a hawk or a crow,

Some small thing beating its heart

Out against the wind. In this life,
No body makes amends.

biographical note

Katharine Coles's fifth poetry collection, *The Earth Is Not Flat* (Red Hen Press, 2013), was written under the auspices of the National Science Foundation's Antarctic Artists and Writers Program; ten poems from the book, translated into German by Klaus Martens, appeared in the summer 2014 issue of the journal *Matrix*. She has also published two novels. Recent poems and prose have appeared in *Poetry Northwest, Seneca Review, Virginia Quarterly Review, Image, Crazyhorse, Ascent*, and *Poetry*. A professor at the University of Utah, in 2009–10 she served as the inaugural director of the Poetry Foundation's Harriet Monroe Poetry Institute. She has received grants and awards from the NEA, the NEH and, in 2012–13, the Guggenheim Foundation. *Flight* is her sixth collection of poems.